GIACOMETTI'S DOG

GIACOMETTI'S DOG

ROBIN BECKER

UNIVERSITY OF PITTSBURGH PRESS

Published by the University of Pittsburgh Press, Pittsburgh, Pa. 15260
Copyright © 1990, Robin Becker
All rights reserved
Baker & Taylor International, London
Manufactured in the United States of America

Library of Congress Cataloging-in-Publication Data
Becker, Robin.
Giacometti's dog / Robin Becker.
p.   cm. — (Pitt poetry series)
ISBN 0-8229-3636-4. — ISBN 0-8229-5428-1 (pbk.)
I. Title.   II. Series.
PS3522.E257G5   1990
811'.54—dc20   89-39342
                                                    CIP

I gratefully acknowledge the following publications in which some of the poems in this collection first appeared: *The Antioch Review* ("Living in the Barn"); *The Cambridge Chronicle* ("Fable," under the title "Fable for Cambridge"); *5 AM* ("The First Summer of the Word Processor," "Good Boy," "Letter from Your Father," "Sadness in Spring," "The Taj Express," and "The White Place"); *Harvard Magazine* ("Floating Farm," "A Marriage," and "Prelude"); *Hawaii Pacific Review* ("The Children of Siran Darda" and "Tantric Pictures"); *The Nebraska Review* ("Philadelphia, 1955"); *New Virginia Review* ("Birch Trees," "Riding Lesson," and "Still Life"); *Ploughshares* ("Bodies We Will Never Know"); *A Poem in a Pamphlet* ("Osteoporosis"); *Prairie Schooner* ("The Children's Concert," "In Pompano Beach, Florida," "On Vashon," and "The Problem of Magnification"); *Science, Technology & Human Values* ("My Father's Heart," under the title "Medical Science," and "The Round Barn"); *The Seattle Review* ("Susan Longmire: The 1891 Ascent of Mt. Rainier"); *Sojourner* ("Incarnate," Rome of the Imagination," "Selective Memory" and "The Subject of Our Lives"); *The South Dakota Review* ("Hiking Gold Hill Ridge"); *Yarrow* ("The Hand-Carved Chairs").

"Living in the Barn" and "My Father's Heart" (under the title "Medical Science") also appeared in *An Ear to the Ground: An Anthology of Contemporary American Poetry* (copyright © 1989 by the University of Georgia Press).

I wish to thank the Massachusetts Artists Foundation and the National Endowment for the Arts for fellowships which aided me in the completion of this book.

I am grateful to the MacDowell Colony, Inc., the Michael Karolyi Memorial Foundation, the Helene Wurlitzer Foundation of New Mexico, and the Massachusetts Institute of Technology for support.

I am indebted to the poets and writers who read the manuscript and helped me put this collection together: Martha Collins, Debra Gorlin, Miriam Goodman, Marea Gordett, Susanna Kaysen, Leslie Lawrence, and Carole Maso; to Nicholas Altenbernd, Helena Bentz, Sally Greenberg, Deborah Kass, and Marianne Weil, many thanks.

*The publication of this book is supported by grants
from the National Endowment for the Arts
in Washington, D.C., a Federal agency,
and the Pennsylvania Council on the Arts.*

To my parents,
Anne Dee Becker and Benjamin Bruce Becker
and in memory of my sister,
Jill Wendy Becker

Contents

I

II

Contents

GIACOMETTI'S DOG

I

The Problem of Magnification

Today after class, my student explains to me
how he and his roommate plan to trap
history between two enormous mirrors they will install
in space. He is particularly interested in sixteenth-century
explorers, coastal South American countries,
wooden boats circumnavigating the globe.
Kindly, my student instructs me in the development
of laser technology, he persuades me with heroic accounts
of electromagnetic radiation, fabulous as any resurrection.
History, he says, is all matter,
and matter cannot be destroyed. A lasso of light sparks
from his chalky fingers as he describes the problem of magnification.
Today you would lose the fine hairs on Magellan's arms,
the grain in the wood of his mast. Soon, he assures me, technicians
will perfect the lens, the light will refract,
and the boys will see the trees of Tierra del Fuego
as they appeared to the Portuguese commander.
Tonight my student and his roommate elucidate the elegant equations.
Their dormitory room is a planetarium
of faith, earth a lonely place, miles from anywhere,
a penciled circle on the small schematic diagram.

Living in the Barn

for Marianne Weil

Beside you in the truck, I almost forget
you are a woman, thirty, turning the wheel,
slamming the door. You could be a boy, fifteen,
slim and eager for exercise in a soiled shirt and jeans.
By the time you closed the deal, the animals were gone,
but their ghosts raise their heads as we pass.
Black and white cows reclaim the pasture; curious billy goats
eye two women rattling up the drive. Like an archetypal barn
from memory, the barn slumps broad and red in the rain.
Now the great hayloft holds your bed and table.
In dreams, the farm boys bale and hurl their burdens
into the atrium; I feel the heavy hooves of Clydesdales
stamping in their stalls; the walls still hold their scent,
their hairs, their troughs, their significant sighs.

You have restored yourself by restoring this barn—
long days under the sun's hot hand,
hours at the drafting table—
planning for the time you would have what you need:
a place to work, a place to live.
Like barn swallows high in the rafters
your sculptures float and fly, wings beating against weathered wood.
In the studio, your welding tools assume the shapes
of fantastic creatures, the bronze and brass of your trade.
You lace your boots, tie back your hair,
prepare for work like a farmer whose animals,
like a ring of friends, surround her.

The Hand-Carved Chairs

Beneath shadows cast by Taos Mountain
grasshoppers ravage the field. All night
we hear them buzz and hiss; by morning
the wheat has vanished, the meadow bald as rockface.
My sons refuse the land, the heat,
the devouring insects. They save their dollars
for motorbikes and ride the rutted roads helmetless,
wild as the children of drunks and beggars.
Forgive me, grandfather. We sell off the land
lot by lot and the Rio Grande rugs that bring a good
price from the Anglo traders. In school, our boys
sat in hand-carved chairs
hurled into the incinerator the day
metal ones arrived by truck from Texas.
Two of my children have already perished
on the Santa Fe Road. Two have settled in Velarde
where they drink and beat their wives.
Their children come to me after school
and my house fills with their wants.
Only Ruben, the youngest, refuses to live or die.
He follows me around the house
like the boy he was ten years ago, unbecoming
in a man. When I find a twenty-dollar bill on the road
I press it to his palm. No words. He will buy the paints
he loves and sit in the ruined adobe facing the mountain.
The days of August drop like ripe apricots.
I gather as many as we can use, the rest rot in the road
smearing orange nectar on the soles of our shoes.

The Accident

Because you were in Navaho Nation, which is a nation within a
state within a nation, there is nothing you can do. He stood
silent, eyes averted, waiting, and when the authorities came, he
did not give his name, address, or reason for slamming you clear
across the highway from behind. You've gathered clay from
every county in the state and trusted the magic of feathers,
bone, deer hoof, animal hair. At the pueblos, in the terrible heat,
you listened to the drums, penitent, sweat pouring down your face.

But he has no insurance, and the tribal elders and the lawyer
from the BIA explain that everyone needs a car or truck in New
Mexico, insurance isn't mandatory, you were on Indian land.
When you tell me the story, you've changed the point of view.
No longer victim, you've become a witness to the accident, to
the slaughter of the Indians, to the years of food stamps and
lousy jobs. In Shiprock, New Mexico, you stand in his shadow,
the only shaded spot for miles.

Bodies We Will Never Know

Cottonwood tufts fill the air like moths;
we rub our eyes in the filmy atmosphere
thick with white dreams, while down the road
at the Sagebrush Inn, a Seeing Eye dog sleeps
beneath the piano where his mistress practices
Linda Ronstadt's greatest hits.
Afternoon. The room is empty
except for the bartender swatting at flies.

On the plaza, tourists lunch in the shade
of the cottonwoods, watching the locals.
The bodies we know grow old in the sun and wind.
The bodies we will never know
contain a perpetual fire
unforgettable as raspberries in winter.

The low adobe wall encircles the house,
a woman's arm falls lightly around your waist.
Right now on the mesa, the cactus blooms—
yellow petals on a blue bone.
Right now on Taos Mountain
the sun discloses the bodies of the boys—
caught in a sudden storm last fall—
who slept above tree line all winter.

The Lover of Fruit Trees

for Henry Sauerwein

The desert of northern New Mexico
stretches behind the garden,
punishing cactus in a hot blue bed.
Civilization begins with the Russian olive
and the Chinese elm.

This year all the trees are full.
Early apricots cluster, and greengage
plums dapple the adobe wall.
We walk what you call your English garden
for its wild and unlikely flowers.

You call them by their Latin names
like the strict uncle who wants to be firm
but loves his brother's children for their flaws.
One blazes bright in the morning and wilts by noon;
another flowers before its time.

We turn to the orchard, your prize,
and I think of the stubborn Jews
who, throughout my childhood, made oranges
grow in the desert. *A miracle,* my father would say.
You understand? A miracle.

Twilight. You reach for your hose
and water disappears into the sandy soil.
Inside, you show me an oversized book
of photographs taken in the Warsaw ghetto
before everything beautiful burned.

My Father's Heart

My father's heart is on television
at the hospital. Lonely and a little embarrassed, it beats blindly on
the videotape, hoping for the best. Like family
members of a game-show contestant, my mother and I
stand off to the side, proud of the healthy culvert doing its chores.
The doctor explains that this is the artery of
a much younger man, and I think of the parts of my father's
body assembled in a shop from the odds and ends
of others. Now the doctor is speaking
very quickly, as if she could hide
the sad blocked door of the right ventricle,
unable to pass its burden of blood
from one room to another. When the lights go on,
I expect to see it, sore and swollen, counting
off the seconds with its bad arm. My mother
takes a few steps, respectfully, holding
her pocketbook, waiting to be addressed. We have seen
the unshaven face of the heart, the cataract
eyes of the heart, the liver-spotted hands
of the heart. Seated in the cafeteria, my mother whispers
that my father's heart is a miracle, that it has already
been dead and recalled twice.

In Pompano Beach, Florida

Like the inflatable palm tree I gave to my lover,
the palm trees on this golf course whisper
eternal life. A man circles the green and kneels,
divining meaning. He knows the sand
trap and the skein of water with its drowned elements.
I consider his handicap, the fast condition
of the course, the way his partners pause to watch,
like couples gathering on the floor
for a slow dance. Sun on his pastel sweater. Sun
on the roofs of rented cars heading to the beach.

My father passes behind me, assembling his orange, knife,
plate, coffee cup. We do not speak, we respect the old lesions,
thick scar tissue; he takes the kitchen,
leaves me the deck. He is frightened he will die
at the Humana Hospital, out of sight, behind the row
of condominiums and the swimming pool.

Last night, after dancing at J.J.'s Otherside,
we listened to the water
clean itself, traveling along its plastic arteries.
And I awoke to the sound of emergency
in paradise, sirens at six A.M., parting the traffic,
the early runners, the golfers and sleepers
still dreaming of a perfect shot at heaven.

Osteoporosis

for my grandmother, Laura Weiner

Awake, you wonder how to turn,
if your muscles will obey your wishes,
or if the porcelain bones, thinning
with each breath, have grown
insupportable overnight.

At the sink, you pencil in your eyebrows—
mindful of your steady hand, even here
in elderly housing, where the dispossessed
have lost memory,
that transparent muscle.

On Broad Street, trolleys screech and wheeze
like frail men at the back of the synagogue.
Powder. Lipstick. Rouge.
You buckle the brace that trusses
your torso like a dancing partner.

Across the hall, Mr. Weiss fumbles
for his keys. You hear
the knock of his metal walker, three
rubber shoes striking
the floor in a waltz step.

Now you may join the others
in the clamorous dining hall.
Already they are pulling out their chairs,
preparing to recite
the blessing before the meal.

Philadelphia, 1955

All the lights are on
in the house of my childhood.
A figure passes behind a window.
Then another with busy hands. Someone
is sick. Someone dials
a telephone.

A child in a nightgown
closes the door and walks barefoot
on the black grass. Stars have grouped
like families into their fixed relations.
She welcomes the great indifference
of the street and recites the names

of everyone asleep in the brick row houses.
Pleasure on her tongue, syllables
follow one another into place.
She whispers to fences and mail slots,
to screen doors, to bicycles tossed
on summer lawns.

She sits in the permissive dark,
a guest unwilling to relinquish
silhouettes of buildings, the cold
concrete against her thigh.
Everything that is her own is suddenly here
revealed, separate as her body

from the house with its lights
and troubles mounting the stairs.
Oh wild and tentative solitude, so new,
so graceless. How can she carry it
from the spacious night back to the distressed
and loving people of her life?

The Return

At night he is returned to me—
a small dog with black eyes—
and his tongue stripes my face
pink, the color of his tender
underbelly. We laugh, we weep,
to find each other again.

Cobwebs shine bright as stars
in the forest. I kneel to feel
his fur against my skin, his satin ears,
the fine bones of his skull
returned to me.

In the Sangre de Cristo we run
through paintbrush and columbine.
I follow him into streams where small stones
glitter in his wake. Past larkspur and penstemon,
he fills the woods with his happiness.

When he lies down, I take him in my arms,
a small stillness returned to me, my everlasting stone.
A shovel is waiting. I dig, again, in the dark wood,
as this is my share, to dig and make a place for him
before the light divides us again.

Like Breath at Your Ear

The light that stabs the blue carpet is familiar, concentrated.
You hunch at your desk writing a paper
for junior English, still wearing your school clothes.
Your mother has gone to the market, your sister is having
her lesson. It is the first warm afternoon in April
in Philadelphia, where you have spent every spring
squinting beneath your desk lamp. Outside dogs graze hedges
and catch new shoots in their wiry hair. You are still so far
from the simplest destinations; knowing this makes you slow down
and stare out the window as if you could conjure
your best friend, working on her paper across town.
You flop onto the bed and a voice comes into the room.
She tells you to take off your skirt.
With indifference, the voice instructs your hand
and you are surprised at how the words move you
up and down on the bed, and how the phrases press your stomach
into the sheets. You have never heard this timbre
in a voice before. Like breath at your ear, the air whirls
electric against your skin, chords vibrate in your arms
and you know you will grow up listening for this woman.
The voice blows syllables and you utter them now, with her, as though
there had always been two worlds, and you'd inhabited that
other one, calling and breathing across a vast and private space.

The Children's Concert

Once a month when I was twelve
     and my sister was ten
our mother would drop us at
     The Philadelphia Academy of Music

for the Saturday children's concerts.
     We'd sit in the enormous dark
hall with the other children and I'd
     whisper to my sister

that our mother was never coming back,
     that she'd abandoned us there,
that she was driving to meet our father
     and take a plane to Europe.

My sister called me a liar
     and her eyes filled
with tears. The musicians had started
     on Mozart, but I was whispering

about how we would feel when all the other
     children had gone and we
were left standing in our navy winter coats
     on the grim Philadelphia street.

I did not know then that I would grow
     to love the eighteenth century,
that my sister would take her own life
     one winter day in Philadelphia,

that childhood could be so final a thing.

The Compassionate Friend

for Tom and Jean O'Hare

In the stoppered night, in the night of the short
sentences and the sharp staccato tears, someone manages
to open her mouth, to tell us—
we who have outlived our children—about the deaths of children
under the wheels of cars, from the plagues of our time,
from overdose and hanging, from the freak
avalanches and mechanical failures.
Each one takes a turn
holding the precious name and the facts
and passes them hand-over-hand like people passing
buckets of water in a line to a burning house.
After a story is told it finds its way back,
night of the parched throat,
and we take it back.
We think the room can't hold so many dead
children but here is the father who visits the cemetery
each day and the mother who refuses to let
her other children leave the house and the sister
who hears her sister calling from the grave.
Is there a poetry for the parents
of the suicide's rope and ladder, a poetry
of vigils in hospital corridors,
a poetry for the mute measures
taken over and over in the final never-ending hours?
Traveling north, I see an animal trotting
along the ditch at the side of the road.
It is the fox, my old friend, starving this time,
his black and red sides heaving. He lifts his head to get
the scent of his pursuer,
and the headlamps of his eyes shine with compassion.

Sadness in Spring

Today I thought about how everyone I know
is sad, how amazing that the forests and deserts
and plains can hold us as we get up and walk
from one season to the next.
In spring all sadness is
wet and branching, sucking at shoes,
and the anniversaries of deaths
are like tiny tombstones on the trails.
Summer is still so far away, not like our dead who stand
in the woods all night, a few feet from the house.

Selective Memory

Light fills the great spaces
behind government buildings in Washington, D.C.

I'm in love, standing outside the National Gallery
and I'm in love again in Dupont Circle.

How delicately two people reacquaint themselves with passion,
each coming from her separate life, focused as a narrow canyon

or a dim street in New York, walking that boulevard
of engagements that is daily life. What I have never managed well

is part of me forever, a friend lost to suicide
or the sadness of family life. And now my body wants to live

alongside yours, as you stood in the hospital room with me
where I had come to hold my grandmother's hand. You were right;

we have to let go of the future the way I let her go back
to her bed. Days later, in the Blackwater Reservation, snow lit

the trails we skied. The argument we were having
comes back to me like the habit of fear. When I tell

how we met, my memory is selective, looking for the words
to tell the best story, though the one that is true is more difficult

to tell, because it leaves everything open.

II

The Round Barn

I wonder if the horses balked
at the curvature, anticipating
clean, indigenous right angles.
They must have paced the perimeter
like their Chinese forbears, circling
the shafts that powered the mills
in the Han dynasty.
And did the farmer mourn the end
of linear thinking, did he pause
to consider the rectangles
of daily life? Haystacks, windows,
narrow rows of corn
in their righteous beds.

Good farmer, when you broke
with your neighbors and led
your livestock into the center
of the cosmos, were you only
following a hunch: that the wind
would sweep around
the progressive curves,
that revolution would harbor you?
Perhaps you saw in the repetitions
of history the wandering Mongolian
sleeping naked in his yurt,
who knew the world was a simple sphere
with an opening at the top for God.

Tantric Pictures

We speak secret, he said. *Kundalini, very good,*
and he left me with the child painting
faces on puppets. Bhaktapur's Durbar Marg

was crowded with tourists, and tour buses
jabbed the marketplace like spears.
I'd biked from Katmandu, asking directions

every few miles to stay on course, stopping
for Cokes. That day the streets were lined with
uniformed schoolchildren paying homage to the queen

of England, making a royal stop.
Long Live Friendship of England & Nepal, the roadside
banners advertised. My shopkeeper returned,

paintings rolled under his arm. *Look,* he said
with great sweetness, unwrapping a blue figure having
most complicated intercourse with a woman in red.

And here, he said, touching his chest. *Oh yes.*
Men and women boxed for shipping, genitalia
prominent. *Tantric, tantric,* he whispered,

holding up Krishna and Ganesh in impossible postures
with gymnastic ladies from Hindu myth. *Very good
price,* he said. *Special for the queen's visit.*

Though the pantheon was limited (no men
with men, no ladies licking), I bought four pictures,
to my friend's great pleasure, and we parted

bowing, bringing our palms together in the Nepalese
style which means, in every village square,
The God in me salutes the God in you.

24

The Children of Siran Darda

Like statuary, the village kids stared
from the ridge. Sister carried little brother
like cordwood on her back.
Twins repeated against the mountains, their poor shirts
fluttered when the wind came up.
Like shiny bullets, one hundred toes
pointed at my tent.
What could I offer to make them go away?
Photos of their mothers squatting in rice fields?
They stepped forward, carrying mantra papers
and copper images of Shiva. They were guarded
against lightning and fear.
They came forward. Earrings helped their ears
hear dharma, the bronze pagodas of their hearts were sacred.
They stepped forward with their soiled palms
and filthy nails. With their hands
outstretched they came.

The Taj Express

The world is a bridge, pass over it but build no house upon it.
—inscription inside archway at Fatehpur Sikri

When the rickshaw drivers wake
they begin the repetitive movements
for which they are famous
and which diminish them, until they are
the size of children
asleep on the landing at platform two.
Before the first train to Agra
the homeless are at home; a woman
boils water, a man folds betel nuts
into edible leaves, someone prays.
Traveler, the gray shapes shifting
at your feet and the huddled bodies
are living and dying on this platform.
They watch you leave with the others
for the Taj Mahal and all day they wait.
When you stand before the minarets
and the marble dome, they arrive selling postcards
and miniature mausoleums. They will take your picture
before the watercourse stocked with fish.
They will lead you to Akbar's deserted city
where an entire civilization died of thirst.
You book a compartment, you think
you can lose them, but they're back at the station
on platform two. This time, they want nothing—
not the air you breathe, not the space you claim,
not your guidebook to their country,
not your second-class passage through this life.

On Vashon

You circle the island in your pickup
calling softly for the dog.
Across the country, I see fog
wrapping the fir trees and rotting wharves
like a gauze bandage.
Chinese in narrow boats
have cast their nets for the last time,
abandoning bowls and pigs.
The harbor fills briefly with canoes
and they are gone.

You look to the east where the Cascades
rise like Tibetan holy lands
and the hanging lakes glow, pale monasteries
in the glacial cirques.
You pass the truck which will carry tomorrow's
flowers to Seattle and the long rows of glass
greenhouses where they do the forcing.
Before dawn someone will cut the stems
and pack them tight. Tonight the dog limps
from the bushes, one paw aloft, an offering.

Good Boy

Small companion,
sometimes I think I see you stir

from your pallet on the floor
and in the moment before the mind

rights itself, I call your name
the way I said it to myself the night

I lifted you from the street
knowing everything would be different.

Blame is as useful as a broken chain,
as the decision I made day after day

to let you run free. Free, you lay
on the rain-stricken street

silver-eyed, without breath,
black curls tight against your perfect chest.

The vet said it was quick, your unmarred body
dying on the inside, all the organs crying together.

Dog of the many days, of the city, of the desert,
I hear the jangle of your collar in my dreams.

I see you standing on the stairs
or racing down the hill, explaining in your best way

that you want to come too, that you'll be a good boy,
that you remember everything I ever taught you.

Riding Lesson

Some days he lurched around
the ring, yelling in Irish. You circled him, he was
the sun, his name was Mick. With his long
whip, he cracked the indolence at your heels,
he made your spine sing its straightest song.

He was a drunk and cast a smelly shadow
while you sat soaping bridles in the tack room
where stirrups took the sun.
Your mother came at six, shafts of light
still hitting the roof of the Impala.

You stood on two hay bales and stared
as they paced in their stalls
wearing bright blankets stained with liniment.
A horse's breath formed a little
white cloud like a man's.

They had the same yellow teeth, the same
lathery sweat. You never knew
when they would turn. At Christmas
your father gave him a bottle, the paddock froze
and the water in the bathtub outside the barn.

After his car wreck, he sat in a plastic
chair and watched the lessons.
With his wet smile. His gimpy leg.
He snapped a crop, he cursed the air,
and then the city closed the stable.

He put the reins of a horse in your hands.
His laughter followed you and made you cry.
Crybaby! He was your first teacher.

Still Life

A bear sleeps in the empty
cabin at the edge of the field. When he rises to
stoke the fire, his brown bulk takes up all the space.
I think of him as a chore, my large, retarded
brother who has never left my parents' home.
He dwarfs their living room furniture with his great
movements, and his enormous appetite
causes my father to work overtime and to drive
home in the terrible sleet.

They shop in malls for clothes that fit
my brother who grows a size each month and wears
out the orange work boots with the tire-tread
soles within three weeks. He does not understand
the ice storm which has glazed each branch
with a clever patina. When he steps
onto the thin surface, he falls through, climbs
up and lurches into the forest, where the
small trees shine with such importance

that he grasps the luminosity and is bathed
in sense, his gigantic feelings filled with light.

Incarnate

I spot him at the water's edge with his daughter, a revised child
from his new, corrected family. Waves roll in and cover my
father's feet; waves tumble the heavy brown shoes of brokerage,
precarious place settings, camp trunks stuffed with our old
clothes. In his mind, my father places each one of us on a
separate beach, a shaman scattering the poisons.

He grasps the child's hand. He has become the family man my
mother always wanted, dreaming up improvements he will make
around the house. When he sees me, he asks forgiveness in a
voice he has discovered since he was my father. "Sure," I say.
"Sure, Dad." I can see that he is happy and I weep; when he
was ours, he hated beaches, he hated being seen. Now he walks
like an Old Testament king, splendid David or great King Saul,
wise with pain.

Letter from Your Father

We dismantle the rooms,
dividing the objects
we have lived among.
Your father, loving
and ignorant, writes to me—
the importance of good health
and family, a garden,
the proximity of his children.

This big man set a place
for me at his table, and I was met
at the door like any child,
though I, a woman, loved
his daughter and arrived
with my hair cut short
and with manners and speech
foreign to him.

In his fine handwriting
your father has called me
his own. And what shall I
call you?

The First Summer of the Word Processor

The old Victorian houses offer their evening portraits—
a woman brushes her hair, someone reads, someone practices
a violin and the sweet sound descends to the street.
I tear a branch from the forsythia bush
flowering on the lawn, my annual theft.
The woman I loved used to scold me for stealing
flowers, broken pot shards, important minutes.
Each year we left town just as the tulips opened,
riding our bicycles onto the ferry.
This May, she tells me, she will dismantle the new machine
and set up shop in a cottage by the water.
The tiny green figures will flash, necessary and mysterious
as love. Summer again. The scent of lilacs.
When it was over, I helped her pack the car,
heaving the old typewriter into the trunk.
Tonight the forsythia glows in my hand, a perennial magic,
a wand of yellow and perishable light.

Prelude

Your torso will lengthen, thin, become as smooth
as a bark canoe moving effortlessly over bodies
of water I will never know.
When you meet friends one by one
you will tell the story
of how we tried to live on air
that thickened year after year.

You will hear that I have left
for that junction of mountain and desert.
There, I will try to carry what I need
on my back, and I will fail.
This will be a period of singing
songs of longing like the canyon wren,
whose diminishing call echoed all summer.

Floating Farm

On summer nights
the horses sleep standing in the fields.
Their stalls are so empty your dream sweeps
like a good groom into the vacant rooms
to check the flooring of wood chips,
the salt licks attached to the walls
like magnified amulets.

Bales of hay cinched
at the waist fill the loft like tawny packages.
Saddles rest in their stands
like swans asleep on the pond.
And released from its duties
the scoop in the grain bin
is the ghost of your hand.

The horses are sleepwalking
in their designated fields.
Before dawn they'll drift—
one sleek shoulder at a time—
to the paddock, to the cool stillness
of the stable, while your dreaming lips
make the syllables of their names.

Susan Longmire:
The 1891 Ascent of Mt. Rainier

I was thirteen years old.
We walked on luminous glaciers
and stared down deep crevasses
where ice caves formed.
At night the Indian guides smoked kinnikinnick
and I dreamed that I was kidnapped
by a Nisqually prince who lived
with his tribe beneath the pale blue glacier.
In a cavern he named me *Avalanche Lily*.

Snow fell quietly as we marched close
to the massive icefalls.
I studied the birds that tore pine cones apart midair
and the ones that stored spider eggs in bark.
Black-tailed deer preceded us to Rainier.
I longed to stroke the twin fawns
appearing every few days at the edge of our camp.

One night the guides roused us in the dark
and tied us together with rope.
We followed their torches
across snow fields toward the crater.
The sun rose as we climbed the summit
and the ridges below flared with light
like icebergs on a choppy sea.

Hiking Gold Hill Ridge

Our boots pestered stones
on the trail, sending tiny avalanches
earthward. Marmots, stone-colored,
vanished in the rocks as we moved through the forest's
green fretwork of pines, where moss hung
from fir trees like blue goatees.

Above tree line, two deer
paused in the wind and sniffed—
turning slowly as if to calculate
how long it would take
the lightning,
that nonhuman danger, to arrive.

When bare rock spoke to the sky
and thunder replied, the high-country
afternoon dialectic began.
Clouds merged. The alpine lake
filled with current
before a bolt locked sky and ridge,

and we turned back with our fears. Rain fell
like rosary beads, hail rattled our teeth.
Gold Hill, a dream passed among us, disappeared
in bursts of light, and the day turned translucent,
aspens shining like new dimes.
Loose-limbed, we loped down in the steady rain,

happy to take the switchbacks as if we'd scaled the summit,
as if we'd seen the gods of summer and winter laughing
on the peaks, eating bowls of berries and cream.

The Story I Like to Tell

In a drugstore north of Ft. Lauderdale
you stand in line to buy a roll of film, and I'm suddenly
aware of desire, how it fills the body
at inconvenient moments. We stare innocently at the magazines.
We are hours away from making love, months away from summer
in our real home, up north. But here, eighty degrees
in mid-December, reports of bad weather arrive
like messages from a distant star. You know I want you
and you smile, for the inopportune
appeals to you. Come closer. If we can't make love,
I'll tell you a story.
My bedroom opened onto olive trees and grapevines.
It was too hot for sheets. Mornings, she walked naked
around the mill, we drank strong coffee, I watered red
geraniums in the garden. At the sight of my thighs, she gasped.
While Italian cyclists rimmed our hill town,
I swept her with my tongue for hours.

How does it feel? Tales of old lovers, silk beneath denim,
pain and pleasure cresting like a Mediterranean
wave, like the moon slung in a Tuscan window.
Come closer. I know you
like meetings after separations, ambiguous
relations, someone kissing your ear. Let's go
to the beach now; palm fronds quiver on postcards;
pelicans are flying close to shore.
If we can't make love, I'll distract you
with another story
I like to tell, the one set on a distant coast,
in another Romance language.

III

Jazz Festival, France

With the first American notes, we recognize each other, we know
the words to all the songs, we remember Chuck Berry
in our collective American ignorance of history
and we love these black musicians on their twenty-five-day
    European tour
for the rock-and-roll in us, the sit-downs and walk-outs
in us, the hard-earned buck in us, the black and white.
On three stages at once

the drummer works two jobs
back home and turns to wipe the sweat
from his hands, the sax
takes a solo. And the crowd draws from a thousand Gauloises,
a thousand Marlboro stars.
Who's the brother

on the piano?
He's breaking our hearts on stage two.
Like the Allies we've come up
from your beaches, we're here to boogie with the Common Market
in the Roman arena. We're ready
to take on acid rain beneath these ancient olive trees.
We flirt and snap
our fingers at the nuclear arsenals,
in our Levi Strauss jeans we all dance in place

while Herbie Hancock
wields the piano
under Chagall's freewheeling sky.

Giacometti's Dog

He moves so gracefully on his bronze legs
that they form the letter *M* beneath him.
There is nothing more beautiful than the effort
in his outstretched neck, the simplicity of the head;
but he will never curl again in the comfortable basket,
he will never be duped by the fireplace and the fire.

Though he has sniffed out cocaine in the Newark Airport,
we can never trust his good nose again.
He'll kill a chicken in his master's yard,
he'll corner a lamb in the back pasture.
He's resigning his post with the Seeing Eye.

Giacometti's *Dog* will not ask for water
though he's been tied to a rope in Naples
for three days under the hot sun.
Giacometti's *Dog* will not see a vet
though someone kicks him and his liver fills with blood.
Though he's fed meat laced with strychnine.
Though his mouth fills with porcupine quills.

Giacometti's *Dog* is coming back
as a jackal, snapping at the wheels
of your bicycle, following behind in his
you-can't-touch-me-now suit.
Giacometti's *Dog* has already forgotten
when he lost the use of his back legs
and cried at the top of the stairs
and you took pity on him.

He's taking a modern-day attitude.
He knows it's a shoot-or-get-shot situation.
He's not your doggie-in-the-window.
He's not racing into a burning house or taking your shirt
between his teeth and swimming to the beach.
He's looking out for Number One,
he's doing the dog paddle and making it
to shore in this dog-eat-dog world.

Conversations in July

1

She said three towns away the smell of lavender lives for years
in the workman's shirts, like mushrooms in the trained dog's nose.
I said here and pulled some thyme from the rocks.
We didn't say anything. Bats circled in the olive trees.
She loved the broad boulevards of that city by the sea
and the cream-colored hotels. I said I think my father is dying,
he's turning away from the days of the week, he's afraid to talk,
to give anything away. She said the living bend
over the counter to speak with the butcher, she said pass me the wine,
she said where are the matches, she said go get some rosemary
for dinner, there is nothing you can do for him.
I said I want to be faithful.
She said a river splashes at the bottom of the gorge, listen.
We listened. Finally she said I can't imagine living without her.
Then we imagined it: a stone path leads to a stone house,
a whitewashed room with a small fireplace. A cat sleeps on the terrace.
With a wooden spoon she pushed the garlic across the sizzling pan.
She said I still can't imagine it, so I might as well watch
the figs growing fatter on the trees. We identified a few stars.
Shadows fell on the picnic table as the river at the bottom
of the gorge splashed through our lives.
Someone said go get some rosemary for dinner.
Finally the figs were an echo big enough to eat.

2

She said read to me from the guidebook.

I said, in the eighth century, elephants and tortoises upheld the sky.

Griffins guarded sacred trees. The ass played the lyre,

the wolf dressed as a monk. As it should be, she said, go on.

In the twelfth century, the husband pruned his vine in February,

in March he blew on two horns, in May he set off

for the wars, in June he gathered fruit, in July he wore a hat

against the sun, he cut his corn with a sickle.

In August he repaired his barrels, in September he trod on his grapes,

in October he beat acorns from an oak,

in November he killed the fatted pig, in December he gathered fuel.

She said don't forget the one-legged, the dog-headed, the headless

with eyes and mouth situated on the breast.

Don't forget the freaks she said, they were created on the fifth day

and are therefore not in defiance of nature. Go on.

I didn't know you were religious, I said.

Watch, she said and became a fish with a horse's head.

How did you do that? I asked. She winked.

She became a peacock.

I said this isn't really happening.

She said you're right, this isn't really happening.

Chagall

In Chagall's great painting of David and Beersheba
one head contains both faces. A red angel
flies over one eye and a blue angel reads above another.

             Janus could see in two directions
at once, who was coming into the house and who
was leaving. He stood in the doorways and arches
of every Roman city, he blessed the journey
and the return from the journey.

             Love must be a two-headed journey,
terrible and wonderful, coming and going from the porches
and terraces of its desiring
like these bright figures.
Villagers cluster in the corners of the painting,
small sheep and green goats nibble the sky
against the mournful violin's
music of fidelity.

             We raise our several faces when we love—
family, village, woman, beast—
moaning in our technicolor sleep.
For him the store rooms of the heart
were never empty, God's messengers arrived to guide
the action in the story, and we too have arrived
in time to catch the ark, leaving momentarily
through the stone arcade of Genesis
for our wild and blessed exile.

Matisse

The fish at the end of Matisse's long pole
wasn't a fish at all but a piece of charcoal attached
like a brain at the end
of his attenuated line of vision.
They say he wanted to ward himself off,
that large intruder,
so he lengthened the distance between his hand
and his work like Gide's lovers.

Between the life you plan to desire
and desire, figs ripen, someone orders café au lait, she is
so elegant in her summer cottons
against the boughs of the plane trees.

How like a life a still life can be:
color in a bowl or movement
through a window. Not the promiscuous
fruit, the fickle wind, but a created thing.

When I depress this button
I hear our promissory
words exchanged to ward off loneliness, forgetting, others.
What I see more or less clearly
is the black-and-white outline of days
numbered with summer months, projected and enlarged
by distance like Matisse's hieroglyphics,
remote on a white wall and filled with restraint.

The White Place

for Georgia O'Keeffe

Bands of gray and rose bind Time in stone.
Easy to lose yourself
among enormous white tears
of spiraling rock.
You walked here, swallows left their tracks
in the air.

The Indians say, "He has heard the coyote bark,"
when a man surpasses others
in understanding.
You dressed in black & white
that your own body might become
an absence.

No clouds filter the sun's ultraviolet
and exacting heat. There are scientific
explanations for
the particular clarity of light

found at eight thousand feet
in the southwestern desert. I want
the desert with nothing interfering,
to know that everything
with the capacity to burn has burned
and burned back to itself.

A canyon wren dead on the trail.
No more or less than sandstone
turning to chalk
in my hand. But animals lure us
to feeling, bird calls and stray dogs
return us to ourselves.

Late summer. The coyote sings every night
and the harp inside me resonates.
I think of the gestures of certain women
who reflect light, saturated
with themselves, composed and
moving to further composure.

47

Decoupage

Broken in half with a great silence at the center—
a French summer day in the south.
Here the gardeners shape
bushes into ramparts, shape the cypress
into a pencil, it's called *tailler*, to cut or prune.

When the waiter comes to the table
I'm grateful
for the infrastructure of speech, the *s'il vous plaît*
of introduction, the trustworthy interrogative
qu'est-ce que c'est?
This language teaches you to think

politely, as in, you don't part
without inviting reunion—*au revoir*—or accept
thanks without dismissing
the need: *je vous en prie.*
And then the day cracks
open and teaches you to pause
by suddenly falling
silent, the last thing you hear
is *bon appétit* before the last person
on the street pedals around the
corner. I fell asleep
last night to music drifting
from the Bastille celebration.
Desire threaded through the dancing crowd
like smoke, like smoke you could smell it
in everyone's hair; it rose from the syntax

of *excusez-moi* and *vous êtes seule?*
You would have liked the string of lights
above the bandstand. They sparkled on and off
in a curious dialogue
with the stars. I want to listen
to them, to you,

as a child, hearing a beloved voice
is calmed

by the little boats of speech,
unmistakable motors,
and the great lake of meaning
into which she will wade.

A Marriage

Diving nude into the pond they made—
the woman first, then the man.
Their dog barks. I am the friend,
I've come up the long driveway with my bottles of wine, good bread,
                  my persistent need for their table.

My friends swim slowly back and forth across the pond
                across the diminishing shafts of light
lingering, lingering, like people at a table, unable
to let go. The good black-and-white dog shakes himself dry.

There is a sadness in our quiet walk
to the house, in the way he reminds her of some small chore
they must do after dinner. The dog finds her hand
and her palm rests on his spotted head. I watch them, loving them,
loving this trilogy of faithfulness renewing itself
with each attention to one thing, and the next.

Tether

Two women sit on a terrace
with plates of lamb, red potatoes, salad.

Their pleasure is a habit
like any other, like toil, like hours

at the desk or shopping in the open market with a basket.
And *entitled* is just a word made real

by action, like *kindness*. The mime troupe that's come
to town practices entering a glass door

on the village green. They prepare and serve
an entire meal with nothing but air.

With their white faces, they are a race of silent
invaders on good behavior, setting an example,

setting invisible tables in whitewashed rooms.
Striped awnings rise all over town. Someone is being shortchanged

at the patisserie; too late, you realize it's you, and now
the dead are knocking to come in, asking

for a place at the table. Like the olive and fig trees
anchoring the terrace, the dead are tethered

to us and we to them, stars and planets in constant
relation like the things we meant

to do or say and those we did. The women talk
and smoke in the last light.

Their bare arms move to the rhythms of their stories
as they pour the dark red wine.

Fable

It was early fall. You rowed me
around the pond
in your ancient boat.
Tart apples lay in a bag with the cheese.
I read you a story
about two women who could not stop
touching each other.
Trumpeter swans paddled close
and you tossed hard French bread
at their black beaks. When you got cold
I gave you my jacket, the leather glistened
like a delicate skin
moving through trees.
You let the oars float
in the oarlocks; you let the boat
drift in circles. You let the women
from the story climb
into the boat. I could not
stop staring. Soon their desire
took up so much room we had to throw
the apples overboard. We had to sit cramped
at one end. Finally we just waded in
and hauled the skiff and the women
to the pier. The story got wet.
The pond was a dark wound.
You unlocked the car and touched
my back, a kindness, as if
I'd always been your lover.

Rome of the Imagination

This time I'm falling in love with a woman
the way Mantegna fell in love with Imperial Rome:

fountains and arches, fragment by fragment, few facts
but lots of feeling. He knew the Rome of his own imagination—

retrospective, hot for the past—like us, awake at night
with our archaeologies.

To him, all Romans were gracious and stately, the city was filled
with temples, she was his beloved Jerusalem.

Rome never betrayed him. He grew old on the streets he painted,
solitary, passionate, a pagan among his fellows.

Grief

It is the kindness of the rabbi I remember now, nine months
after my sister's death. After the funeral, he took me aside
and said, *Call me when your lover arrives: we'll meet at the cemetery
and hold our own service.* The next day we buried her again.

Then it was summer, and I stood, a Jew among the Catholics
of Florence, dropping my lire into the tin box
with the mourners in Santa Maria Novella. My lover watched,
estranged, and I could not explain why I needed to leave the bright

piazzas, climb the steep steps to San Miniato al Monte and walk
beside the dim paintings, down the long naves, past the spectacular
tombs, to light candle after candle in Santo Spirito, Santa Maria
del Carmine, Santa Croce. I paused on a bridge over the Arno

and considered the way Italy resembled a vast cemetery,
generations buried beneath the marble floors of every church.
Like an island in the Venetian Lagoon, her life was
a place I visited by boat, changed each time I arrived on shore.

Now I dream her face, the color of a Bellini masterpiece,
painted when he was old and saw his dead against the dawn
light, blameless, cold. Already the grieving gather the candles
and clothing they need for the seasons of mourning, naming

themselves lover, mother, father, friend, brother, sister.

Built on Water

Before sleep, I return to Tintoretto's Venice:
the intricate surfaces of buildings dissolve
into light flickering on the Grand Canal; waiters, in tails
and late for work, rush to a vaporetto leaving the pier.

In the chilly rooms of the Scuola Grande di San Rocco,
foreshortened figures with temptations and fevers swirl.
For twenty-three years he painted colossal messengers hurtling
from space, Isaac waiting to receive his blow.

They say he loved the human body for itself, so that when Saint Mark
flew down from heaven to free the slave, both men seemed to embrace
the air with their perfect forms. On the steps of San Zaccaria,
you offer me a pomegranate, luminous as molten glass,

and we walk to the market, passing our bottle of sparkling water
back and forth. Like Tintoretto's figures, Venetian boatmen move
through the crowd in their bright shirts, as the dusk comes in from Murano,
travels a fretwork of secret bridges, deceiving reflections.

The Bath

I like to watch
your breasts float like two birds
drifting downstream; you like a book,
a glass of wine on the lip
of the porcelain tub,
your music. It is your way of dissolving
the day, merging the elements of your body
with this body. The room fills with steam
like mist off a river—
as intimate to imagine you
pleasuring yourself: watery fingers, slow
movement into fantasy.
You call me in and take my hand
in your wet hand. I have to shield my eyes
from the great light
coming off your body.
When you ask me to touch you
I kneel by the water like a blind woman
guided into the river by a friend.

Birch Trees

From a distance, they are the perfect sentences
we have been reaching for
most of our lives.
They are like the dead

who remember, coming into a room,
how the room grew large
to accommodate
great feeling.

Today in the rain
pale bark unwinds like tiny white flags
and I think of how people
unwrap one another

over a long time and how they learn
the patience to live
alongside the dead who will not speak
and will not go away.

The Subject of Our Lives

The storm has started and they say it won't stop.
Not for you, hanging on in the office after everyone has left.
Not for the ponies in my friend's paddock, huddled and still
and turning white. I know from your voice that you like
this moment—a Friday afternoon, the city between us, a few hours
of paperwork before you can think of dinner or a movie

or sex. I have been thinking about the snowstorm, and about a woman
from Chicago who put me on skis and ordered me to follow her
into the woods. That was years ago, and I've stopped thinking
about her, except during blizzards, everybody powerless and stuck
without milk or cream. Now I see that love is really
the subject of our lives: the authority with which you opened

your jacket and placed my hand, rigid, near frostbite,
against your breast, waiting for the heat to make its miraculous
leap; the gentle rabbi leading my parents from my sister's grave.
The ponies stir at the sound of grain hitting a metal bucket,
carried by a woman who regulates their hungers. How many times
have I confused hunger and love, love and power? My head ached

for years, it seemed, following someone's beautiful back.
My sister wouldn't sleep or wake beside one person long enough to
learn something. *Trust me,* you say, and I'm struck by the force
of your voice, the imperative form of any verb spoken in bed.
     Come home.
No, stay where you are. Longing will serve us while snow thickens
the sidewalks, delays the subways, tightens every street in town.

About the Author

Robin Becker has won fellowships in poetry from the National Endowment for the Arts and the Massachusetts Artists Foundation. Her poems have appeared in *The Antioch Review, Ploughshares, Prairie Schooner, The Seattle Review,* and other magazines. Her previous collections of poetry are *Backtalk* and *Personal Effects.* She lives in Cambridge, Massachusetts, where she teaches in the Writing Program at the Massachusetts Institute of Technology and serves as poetry editor for *The Women's Review of Books.*

PITT POETRY SERIES

Ed Ochester, General Editor

Peter Meinke, *Night Watch on the Chesapeake*
Peter Meinke, *Trying to Surprise God*
Judith Minty, *In the Presence of Mothers*
Carol Muske, *Applause*
Carol Muske, *Wyndmere*
Leonard Nathan, *Carrying On: New & Selected Poems*
Leonard Nathan, *Holding Patterns*
Kathleen Norris, *The Middle of the World*
Sharon Olds, *Satan Says*
Alicia Suskin Ostriker, *Green Age*
Alicia Suskin Ostriker, *The Imaginary Lover*
Greg Pape, *Black Branches*
James Reiss, *Express*
David Rivard, *Torque*
William Pitt Root, *Faultdancing*
Liz Rosenberg, *The Fire Music*
Maxine Scates, *Toluca Street*
Richard Shelton, *Selected Poems, 1969-1981*
Peggy Shumaker, *The Circle of Totems*
Arthur Smith, *Elegy on Independence Day*
Gary Soto, *Black Hair*
Gary Soto, *The Elements of San Joaquin*
Gary Soto, *The Tale of Sunlight*
Gary Soto, *Where Sparrows Work Hard*
Tomas Tranströmer, *Windows & Stones: Selected Poems*
Chase Twichell, *Northern Spy*
Chase Twichell, *The Odds*
Leslie Ullman, *Dreams by No One's Daughter*
Constance Urdang, *Only the World*
Ronald Wallace, *People and Dog in the Sun*
Ronald Wallace, *Tunes for Bears to Dance To*
Cary Waterman, *The Salamander Migration and Other Poems*
Bruce Weigl, *A Romance*
Robley Wilson, *Kingdoms of the Ordinary*
Robley Wilson, *A Pleasure Tree*
David Wojahn, *Glassworks*
David Wojahn, *Mystery Train*
Paul Zimmer, *Family Reunion: Selected and New Poems*